WARFARE
✠ in Medieval Manuscripts

WARFARE
✳ in Medieval Manuscripts

PAMELA PORTER

5

First published in 2000
This edition published in 2018 by
The British Library
96 Euston Road
London
NW1 2DB

Text © 2000 and 2018 Pamela Porter
Illustrations © British Library Board and other named copyright holders

British Library Cataloguing in Publication Data
A catalogue record for this book is available
from The British Library

ISBN 978 0 7123 5605 3

Designed and typeset by Will Webb Design
Printed and bound in China by C&C Offset Printing Co., Ltd.

Page 2:
A close encounter on the battlefield,
early 15th century.
Harley MS 4431, f. 110.

Pages 4–5:
Knights and archers fight side by side,
late 15th century.
Royal MS 14 E IV, f. 14v.

Page 128
Marching into battle,
before 1483.
Royal MS 18 E I, f. 147.

Contents

Introduction   9

1 THE ART OF WAR   15

2 KNIGHTS, CHIVALRY
AND THE TRAINING
FOR WAR   25

3 KNIGHTLY ARMS AND ARMOUR   39

4 ARMIES AND BATTLE   59

5 CASTLES AND SIEGES   87

6 GUNPOWDER AND THE
DECLINE OF MEDIEVAL
WARFARE   109

Further Reading   123

Index   125

oment le comonne gent. checon leuk agtremuierou   dra autre octne ꝑ le aueꝛ ꝑꞇ met
rꞇe. E ceo est dunt iious esproums bren ꝗ le iour de dreꝗt iugemet for   met aproche.

Introduction

THE WAYS OF WAR in the Middle Ages seem never to lose their attraction. The glamour associated with knights in shining armour, colourful tournaments and heroic deeds continues to have a strong appeal for the modern imagination, whilst the technical ingenuity of mighty war engines and dramatic scenes of battle provide a constant source of awe and admiration. Thanks to extensive exploitation of its image, medieval warfare has managed to acquire something of a colourful impression, making it relatively easy to overlook the fact that war in the Middle Ages would have been no less harsh and repugnant a business than it is today. Modern attitudes have changed, however. Nowadays war is considered in general to be an unwanted and objectionable event in the course of daily life, while in the Middle Ages it played a prominent, if not to say dominant, role in the pattern of everyday existence. Brute force was accepted as the legitimate way of resolving almost any dispute, and military power was employed not only in major conflicts between countries but also to settle an endless succession of

Knights and foot soldiers engaging in battle,
c. 1327–35.
Add. MS 47682, f. 40.

personal and local quarrels – so much so, in fact, that in medieval times warfare was regarded as a profession for the upper classes and the divisions of society were reflected almost as much in the practice of war as they were in the possession of land.

Over time metal corrodes and wood and fabrics decay so that comparatively few pieces of military dress and equipment have survived to provide us with direct insight into the way that war was waged in earlier times. For a truly comprehensive view of the practical details of medieval warfare we must rely on written documentation and the information preserved in paintings, sculptures, carvings and other pictorial sources. This is where manuscripts come into their own, since by far the most numerous visual representations of medieval warfare are to be found in the miniatures and drawings in manuscript books. The chief reason for this abundance is that books have tended to survive in greater numbers than other artefacts by virtue of their having led a sheltered life on library shelves, protected from the rigours of everyday exposure. As an ancillary benefit many of these individual volumes have multiple illustrations to maximise their potential for making a contribution towards revealing the many and varied aspects of medieval military life.

Often extremely evocative, the miniatures in medieval manuscripts can perhaps create the impression of giving a 'snapshot' view of what it was actually like to engage in warfare in the Middle Ages, offering a potentially rich source of information about military dress, equipment and practices, but it has to be remembered that as sources of accurate information they need to be treated with a certain amount of caution. The images certainly portray medieval warfare as seen through contemporary eyes, but we must constantly bear in mind that the principal aim of most medieval book illustrators was not to provide documentary evidence for the benefit of future generations. Representations of military dress and weapons may be recognisable, but in the absence of supporting documentary or concrete evidence it is frequently impossible to know whether the items depicted reflect a degree of knowledge on the part of the artist or simply demonstrate his powers of invention or skills as a copyist. We must also remember that medieval illuminators tended not to show the same concerns for historical accuracy as those we would expect from a modern book illustrator, so well-documented events such as the Battle of Hastings are frequently portrayed in contemporary rather than historical terms, which can be totally misleading. Such considerations aside, the depictions in medieval miniatures, taken comprehensively, can still represent an extremely important source for tracing the broad development of military equipment and practices throughout the Middle Ages.

(overleaf)
15th-century view of the Battle of Hastings, c. 1460–68.
Yates Thompson MS 33, f. 155v.

1
THE ART OF WAR

RULES FOR THE PREPARATION and conduct of warfare in medieval times were guided chiefly by theories inherited from Graeco-Roman antiquity. Classical manuals of military science, containing detailed technical instructions in matters of siegecraft, the construction of war machines, strategy, tactics, and the training of troops, were full of theoretical concepts and applied mechanics which depended heavily on accompanying visual aids for a full understanding of the texts they presented. Byzantine manuscripts written in Greek in the early Middle Ages maintained a continuity with this classical tradition, providing examples of the interdependence of illustration and text. Comparatively few of these earlier Byzantine manuscripts have survived but our knowledge of them is extended by sixteenth-century copies, made at a time when such detailed interest in military theory was enjoying a considerable revival. One such copy, produced in Northern Italy, is known to be a faithful reproduction of an eleventh-century

Floating and standing structures used for attacking a fortress,
11th century, copied in the 16th century.
Add. MS 15726, f. 30.

Greek manuscript which did survive and is now in the
Vatican Library. A manual on poliorcetics, or siegecraft, by
a tenth-century writer known as Hero of Byzantium, it is
essentially a compilation of material derived from earlier
Greek writers which has been modernised by the author
with the intention of making it user-friendly for a non-
specialist public. In keeping with the classical texts from
which it is derived it contains a large number of extremely
detailed 'technical' illustrations to assist the reader's understanding of the complicated techniques and equipment of
siegecraft as described in the text. A comprehensive account
of a mobile siege tower which can be moved in any direction
is accompanied by an illustration showing an eight-wheeled
penthouse or shelter with a ram suspended by strong ropes
from its structure. The battering end of the ram is equipped
with a crossbeam bearing a net to be used for scaling walls,
while an enclosed area above provides a shelter for observing
the defensive measures of the enemy within the fortress. The
entire structure is massive in proportion to the accompanying figures, consistent with the textual comment that it
requires a hundred men to move it on account of its weight.
Another illustration (see page 14) shows two floating structures for attacking and entering a stronghold by sea. In each
case two ships support a platform on which a massive frame
has been constructed. From one a ram, manipulated by two
lightly clad figures, is suspended by strong ropes. This ram
appears to have a dual function, since it seemingly incorpo-
rates an assault bridge to allow entry by an armed invading
attacker through the breach it creates. The rear structure
carries a simple drawbridge for entry over a wall, raised and

lifted by two figures using ropes. Accuracy is underlined by the presence of two heavy busts which act as counterweights to the assault bridges and their operators. The number of illustrations and the scrupulous attention to detail in such books, of which many were produced in the eastern Mediterranean area during the early Middle Ages, give the impression that they were intended primarily for study rather than for immediate practical consultation.

By contrast, the classical tradition of applied illustration seems to have died out completely in the west, perhaps all the more surprising because military thinking in medieval Europe was dominated by the work of Flavius Vegetius Renatus, a high-ranking official of the fourth century AD. His *De re militari* was widely copied, translated and adapted, as witnessed by the fact that over 300 medieval manuscripts of his work still survive, without doubt representing a mere fraction of the total number actually made. Although outdated in many respects, the work included a chapter on siegecraft, a skill vital for the success of many medieval campaigns, and its presence in many royal and noble libraries indicates that it was in all probability required reading for a military commander. As well as luxury copies made for libraries there are still in existence a number of manuscripts in a portable, compact format, suggesting that the work may also have been regarded as useful for reading or consultation whilst on campaign. This could have been the case with a manuscript of Jean de Meun's French translation of Vegetius (see page 27) which is approximately the size of a standard modern paperback and quite well-thumbed. Whatever their format, however, Vegetius manuscripts do

not normally contain any explanatory visual aids to comple-
ment their text. Such pictures as occur – and illustrations
are by no means universal – are typically presentation
miniatures or appropriate generalised subjects such as
knights in combat or siege scenes.

Vegetius cites as one of his sources a theoretical treatise
on military science, later lost, written by another author
popular in the Middle Ages, although of considerably less
importance if the number of surviving manuscripts of his
other known work, *Stratagemata,* can be taken as evidence.
Sextus Julius Frontinus, a Roman soldier and author who
lived from about AD 40 to 103, compiled this collection of
military stratagems from Greek and Roman history,
presumably for the purpose of providing concrete examples
as a supplement to his theoretical manual. The lasting value
of using specific situations to explain the finer points of
military theory very probably accounts for continuing interest in this practical handbook of Frontinus beside the more
abstract work of Vegetius. Surviving medieval copies of the
Strategemata resemble those of the *De re militari* in that
they are sometimes decorated or illustrated with conven-
tional miniatures but do not include what may be termed
'technical' illustrations, apart from one known exception.
The British Library possesses nine leaves from a manuscript
made in Italy sometime in the late fourteenth century,
which consists of a remarkable series of detailed and lively
coloured drawings occupying about two-thirds of each page
below the brief sections of text to which the illustrations
relate (see opposite). Very individual in style, the drawings
portray the situations described in the text and supplement

**An army's defences against
the enemy,**
late 14th century.
Add. MS 44985, f. 1v.

hoste z inipeditiī nūc z maxime equita
tu sup ante consecutus ē z triplice ēcim ē
peditum atē eorum auit. relictis mēta
llis pleuē armaturā z equitē quie in
nouissimo collocauerat. ut cum eos ex

egisset ē mitteret. Tūm post signanis q̄
in secūda atie erant impariit. ut dil
os numerosofq̄ palos firmos in cūm
defigēt in ↄ· z q̄ eos appinqiatibur
quadaugio ante signa niar atē reape.

it in exactly the same way as the technical illustrations of classical antiquity, suggesting that the volume was either modelled on an earlier manuscript or deliberately made to reproduce the antique style. The present location of the remainder of the volume is unknown, if indeed it still survives, and these nine leaves represent only a very small fraction of the whole text. Assuming that the entire manuscript was a complete version and conceived in the same format throughout it would have been a large, grand and very expensive volume, undoubtedly made for a most important patron.

There is little evidence of any attempt to develop the independent study of military technology in western Europe in medieval times until Konrad Kyeser, a German military engineer from Eichstätt in Bavaria who had fought in a crusade against the Turks, occupied himself during a subsequent three years of exile in his home town by compiling a fully illustrated technical manual on the military arts (which for him included magic and astrology). Written in Latin and entitled *Bellifortis*, the work exists in a single presentation manuscript, dated 1405 and now kept in Göttingen University Library, and it is copiously provided with detailed illustrations relating to the technology and war machines discussed in the text. Despite not appearing in print until many centuries later his work evidently caught on in its day, and further manuscript copies, excerpts and amplifications soon began to appear. Perhaps the best-known of these was the 1459 copy of a practical manual commissioned by the German fencing master Hans Thalhoffer as a work of reference,

Detailed representation of a trebuchet from Kyeser's *Bellifortis*, 1459.
Royal Library Copenhagen, MS Thott 290 2°, f. 16v.

now kept in the Royal Library in Copenhagen. Known as Thalhoffer's *Fechtbuch* (fencing manual) it contains not only his own text on fencing but also the text of Kyeser's *Bellifortis* with the appropriate illustrations (see pages 20, 22).

(opposite)
How to set up a scaling ladder,
1459.
Royal Library Copenhagen,
MS Thott 290 2°, f. 21v.

(above)
Donkey operating a trebuchet,
c. 1300.
Stowe MS 17, f. 243v.

Militbus referens suam sic stando figuram
Indulge fidei subiecte respice puram
Mentem desflevam tibi semper ubiqz paritam
Nam dno michi te dnm qa te fore gratam
Esse meum noscas in preiunctis quia cerno
Vexquina virtutes sequeris nuqz tua sperno
Iussa precor dignare preces audire precantis
Sponte tibi uero fidei celo famulantis
Prom mea tibi matre preces cu suplica mete
Porrigo pro Roma genitrice mea no flente
Nuc eget ipa parens tutela nuiqz senatus
Sensato senio rex cuius tu trubeatus
Quondam consul amor quia sensu urbe Senator
Te rogat ut culpe ne crescat flo medicator
Indiget ipa tui presenti conditione

Supplico puate qui regia carmina audit
Hec tua que tradit in miscta pro breuitate
Exaudire uelis que poscat nomine prati
Ut ubi sint qinti inuentes rex pie celis
Leua lausqz deo tibi rex decus noc paritur
Detantiqz detur exime spes magna tropheo
Pres faciendi seu uerbos fato salute
Iusta salus fore qua poscitur ut mala seu
Nuc patrare uytente fi fernido uideatur
Ipa necab dantur sic prelia dum fore miret
El quasi re mim contingere qp meditante
Vnde retardantur nie figent unimeta dica
Pesca completa scdabit bella uetusta
Rumoz tua iusta reddet comota quieta
Non fiunt facile que no in pace petuntur
Donaqz plangantur senio qz iam iuuenile
Tempus ridebat rex dapsilis puis esto
Vt faciaas presto tuus ut pater ipe solebat

Cum manet ancapitmentis luctantis agone
Si uirtute tua quam sperat pace fruetur
Confidas felix qp te fortuna sequetur
Scilicet ipa dei que gra psiera reges
Sublimat siuat letatur condere leges
Sic ego spero quidem timor hinc orietur in orbe
Qui discede longe tu pessime morbe
Plene doli situm te falso putasse pudebit
Et qz qui sequitur tua pessima nota dolebit

2

KNIGHTS, CHIVALRY AND THE TRAINING FOR WAR

THE KNIGHT, the professional soldier of the Middle Ages, is a figure who perhaps more than any of his contemporaries has captured the popular imagination. The striking figure dominating the written page in a manuscript commissioned in about 1335 by the city of Prato in Italy as a gift for King Robert of Naples (see opposite) offers just the type of glamorous image on which the popular knightly stereotype is usually based – a mounted warrior in full armour, equipped with sword and shield and carrying a lance with a pennon. Full military trappings are an essential feature of the knight's outward appearance, but they are probably less likely to account for his intrinsic appeal than the romantic image promoted by his association with the medieval world of chivalry and all its attendant pageantry.

Chivalry was the word used to describe an elaborate code of conduct which determined knightly behaviour. The name came from the French word for mastery of the horse, one of the chief skills that a young knight acquired when he

A knight on horseback, armed and with heraldic trappings,
*c.*1335–40.
Royal MS 6 E IX, f. 24.

received his early training in the arts of war. Although not always strictly followed, the rules of chivalry represented the highest military, courtly and religious ideals. A knight was expected to be valiant in battle and magnanimous in victory, gentle in manners, generous, truthful and just. It was also his duty to protect women, and to show undying devotion to his lady.

Knights came from a particular social class, the training for knighthood starting at an early age when a boy was sent to court to serve as a page. Here he began to acquire some of the skills essential for his later role, in particular those involved in mastering horsemanship. Serious military training started at the age of fourteen, when as a squire he carried his knight's shield, accompanied him to battle, assisted him in putting on his armour and cared for his weapons and horses. At the same time a squire also received regular training for arms and combat.

One illustration to a manuscript of a French translation of Vegetius, whose first chapter deals with the education of recruits, shows a young squire fighting at the 'pile' or 'pale', a device employed to teach the use of the sword and shield during combat on foot (see page 28). The 'pile' sometimes took the form of a Turk or Saracen, but here we find the more usual plain pole, about 6 feet (1.8 metres) high, firmly fixed in the ground and with notches placed to indicate the head, arms and other vulnerable parts of the opponent's body. Another figure in the same miniature is demonstrating the awkward task of mounting a horse when fully armed, one of the knight's most essential and vital accomplishments.

St George as an armed and mounted knight, *c.* 1390–1400. Sloane MS 2683, f. 14v.

Before leading an army into battle a squire had to be knighted, a ceremony which for reasons of expediency might be forced to take place whilst on campaign (see opposite). Otherwise the knighting ceremony occurred when a squire reached the age of twenty-one, as long as he had demonstrated his worthiness to receive the two most potent symbols of knighthood, a sword and spurs. A simple ceremony of giving weapons to the new knight gradually became more elaborate and solemn under the influence of the Church, involving a ritual bath to symbolise purification, a night of vigil and prayer and the blessing of his sword before it was given to the sponsor to whom he made his knightly vow. Sometimes the presentation of weapons was accompanied by the accolade, a symbolic blow on the

(above)
A squire training for knighthood, beginning of the 14th century.
Sloane MS 2430, f. 2v.

(opposite)
Knighting on the battlefield, early 15th century.
Harley MS 1319, f. 5.

shoulder with the flat of the sponsor's sword. At last the knight was ready to play his full part in war and all its related activities.

Much of the pageantry of medieval courtly life was associated with a pastime which provided the knight with invaluable training and practice for the field of battle. The tournament was an entertaining spectator sport in which two teams of knights fought each other in friendly contest to win honour and renown. In the tournament proper or mèlée two teams of knights fought a mock battle according to an agreed set of rules, while the joust – frequently included as part of the programme – was an individual encounter which enabled two knights to display their military skills to best advantage (see page 33). Although the object of the sport was friendly, at least in theory, many early tournaments were rather rough affairs involving indiscriminate mass combat, often leading to death and injury

A knight setting off for war,
early 14th century.
Add. MS 42130, f. 202v.

(see pages 34–35). Later tournaments became more controlled, perhaps because the presence of ladies among the spectators exerted a civilising effect on the proceedings (see page 36). Sometimes the rules allowed the victors to demand ransoms, arranged beforehand, or to capture horses, arms and armour from vanquished opponents, as might happen in reality on the battlefield. At the end of the day there was usually a prize, presented by a lady, for the knight who performed best. Gradually the reduction of physical risk to the participants was emphasised to such a degree with the development of specialised armour and the introduction of safety features such as tilt barriers that by the end of the fifteenth century the medieval tournament with all its skill and excitement had been transformed into little more than a theatrical spectacle. By that time, however, the nature of warfare was changing so significantly with the introduction of new weapons and skills that the role of the knight on the battlefield was already in decline.

(opposite)
The joust as a civilised spectacle, 1470–72.
Harley MS 4379, f. 43.

(overleaf)
An early tournament, more like a battle than a sport, *c.* 1352.
Add. MS 12228, ff. 160v–161.

N celle saison et
entretant que les
trieues se tenoi
ent en france et
en angleterre par mer et par terre
que les anglois et leurs subiectz
se vouloient bien tenir reserue
naine pillars qui estoient en
auuergne Ceulx ainsi de mar
ches herioient le puis et ses poures
gens deca la riuiere de dourdone
dela maie ses souuenement
ppitances qui estoient rendue

que le puis Sauuerine en recep
uoit les plaintes en venoient a
pure eut conseil le roy de fran
ce denuoyer deuers le roy dangle
terre et luy escripre et signifier
tout lestat de ces mauuais pil
lars qui guerre faisoient en ce
puntes et puis enclore en la puy
soubz lombre de leurs metis lagle
chose ne se pouoit ne deuoit bon
nement ne seaument faire En
tretant que ces choses se deme
noient et re croy bien que le roy

ul nel remuent mie de la sele
ul se tient si fermement com
sil fust fermes ensele. mes to
ute uoies. lont ul feru si dure
ment. que il se sent naurez.
mes non mie trop enparfont.
Quant il on lor glaiues
busiez. et il se sent en
sint feruz. porce quil nauoit
point de glaiue. se lance ul
sor missire gau. et giete les
braz. et le prent a heaume
et le tire adonc uers soi si

bronchier de sus laricon te
uant. et poi sen falt. quil
ne chex. mes bbo. qui se se
trop durement chargiez de
celui cop. hurte. tout ma
intenant cheual tes espe
rons et sen passe oltre.
Quant en li erc. grant e
la noise a celui point
encelui endroit. ou li rois ar
tus auoit este abatuz. et li
autre compaignons li bons
chlrs qui se uoit encele pres

enle thyet. li rois mebarous
se mesce sor lui. et fair vne
pointe si aspre. quil fair vo
ler ala terre et lui et le cheual
et lors encomence acrier si
haut com il puet loenoys lo
enoys. et tant fair huc par si
ne force. malgre tous cels q
la estoient. remonte tout to
ut mamtenant le roi pellymo
qui auoit este abatus encele
presse ensint com ge uos ai
conte ca arrieres. lautre chr

ne. li rois mebarous estoit
si durement liez de ce quil li
estoit si bien auenuz aceste
encomencement. que tout li
cors li tresalt de ioie si dist au
roi pellynor. qui uos semble
de nostre comencement de ce
ste iornee. sire fair li rois pel
lynor quant que uos aliez
deuinant e auenuz. si puisso
encor tant faire. quil ne pe
uist reuengier ceste iornee.
ne ceste honte. atone uos se

Patteur sur la venue de ...... Rompure sur les lices

(above)
Ladies witness a knight's downfall in a tournament,
c. 1470.
Cotton Nero D ix, f. 40.

(opposite)
Fighting on foot in the joust,
early 14th century.
Royal MS 14 E III, f. 156v.

en samble.
autune fois
roine te pd
ichestui me
sus acort si
droit appar
rois tei da
chaus q̃ ch

e q̃nt lanc̃. le
voit apie si lui
est auis q̃ sil le
requeroit ache
ual q̃l enseroit
trop blasmes si

genoulle tei
pee. z lui dist
car iou me i
manale z en
q̃ iou nel ti
chenes a si
estes ne me
nir ne a mi
mi portoie
bii moustre

descent z laisse aler son cheual q̃l
pt q̃l veut. puis trait lespee z
griete lescu sour sa teste z bait te
querre mador z lui dõne si grãt
caup pmi le hiaume q̃ tout lestõ
ne. z ne pourq̃nt il se deffent

3
KNIGHTLY ARMS AND ARMOUR

A knight with his horse,
early 13th century.
Royal MS, 2 A XXII, f. 220.

FROM THE NORMAN CONQUEST onwards weapons and basic equipment remained essentially the same, but the appearance of the knight changed in certain distinctive ways as attempts were made to improve the protective qualities of body armour, helmets and shields. Miniatures in manuscripts allow us to document the broad sequence of these developments but we must be cautious when making specific interpretations. First and foremost there is the difficulty of identifying a 'typical' knight at any one moment in time. Responsible for the provision of his own armour, a knight might well have had to consider practical factors such as cost and availability – hard-wearing armour was often handed down within families – so that a wide variety of types and styles could be found side by side at any one point in time. When looking at the illustrations we need to bear in mind that artists were not necessarily recording accurate information either about the armour of their own day or about armour in general, that they may sometimes have been following certain artistic conventions that we do not under-stand, and that a vast amount of copying took place from one source to another. The portrayal of the forged or riveted metal rings used in the making of mail armour provides a good example of the problems. A number of different techniques were used to convey the linking process, implying the exist-ence of a corresponding variety of patterns, but surviving pieces of mail fail to corroborate this. It is quite possible that artists were following some sort of convention, or maybe just finding a way of distinguishing between different groups of warriors or types of armour. In some cases of course the artist may have been familiar with the general appearance of mail but unfamiliar with its mode of construction and so was merely using his creative imagination.

Until the eleventh century, warriors wore everyday clothes with shields for protection, their leaders sometimes adding a helmet and short mail shirt, but a mounted knight needed better bodily defence. On horseback it was not only awkward to manoeuvre a shield, but an opponent's weight combined with the speed of his horse would greatly increase the force of any blow. Consequently the mounted knight differed from his predecessors in wearing a mail shirt and protective mail coverings for his limbs, while the addition of a helmet became the norm. The mail shirt or hauberk reached midway down the thigh with a slit up the fork of the legs to accommodate the saddle (see page 38). Worn over a thin gown the hauberk, with a few refinements, remained the main body defence throughout the twelfth century, but in later years the knight's appearance took on a new look with the introduction of a long loose gown worn

Mail-clad knights at war, 1225–50.
Lansdowne MS 782, ff. 31v–32.

lun mozcur lautre chair ebruch   & ke le bon rei pncipal

Qnt il se peent tristur apuier   ke si niebs ki teneie durendal

ke austrean funt tut lur esperlast   oi eri le bon duc naturial

Tute la place lur unt fait uoider   & le barnage de france lerial

vers lestandard les ueillez chacer   Sore lur couvent al entree du mal

Austricans pernet al rei aofiler   lancent etraient e funt tel batestel

Si cel uut peont apmer   seo ken divroie car tant iour for mal

Ja lestandard neu aua meft   La su lestur doler e champial

veit Id nour ke conucer   Cil dorphanie un people deseal

& uere sa gent de sur lui achac   Si deu nenpense le pere espirital

Si ne lur peot socure ne aider   Vnc na conueret tant dolerus iornal

Had sur ciel rei ke tant se face fier   Cil de orphanie se sunt arestux

Se li neist sa gent aparler   & hadal e pantalis sil danz

ke lui dust de pite ennuier   Devant la roche se sunt defenduz

Sunt estandard neot un poi delaer   la ueisez tant cop teruz pesant

or uerez Galidze ne su mie cultun   copees testes espaules e buz

Il maudia ke li fist comencer

over the armour. A thirteenth-century illustration to a 'Chanson' relating to the wars of Charlemagne shows how a tight-fitting mail hood known as a coif was made as one with the hauberk to protect the head (see page 41), while by this time mail 'mittens', slit at the wrist to free the hand for normal use when not in combat, had appeared on the ends of the sleeves.

Although flexible enough to allow relative freedom of movement and effective against sword cuts, mail must have chafed the skin, even with an undershirt, whilst offering only minimal protection against heavy blows. Foot-soldiers, normally unable to afford mail armour, wore more home-spun protection in the form of a quilted tunic fashioned from two pieces of material padded with wool, cotton or rags. Known as a gambeson or aketon, this garment was difficult to pierce and remarkably effective in deadening a blow. From the early thirteenth century onwards the well-equipped knight added a similar quilted garment as a shock absorber under his hauberk, a safety feature which also added greatly to his comfort. Some warriors wore garments with protection for the upper part of the body in the form of overlapping riveted plates – a type of scale armour, usually worn as an alternative to mail and particularly popular in the thirteenth century. Iron or horn plates, either rectangular or with rounded ends, were attached to a cloth or leather garment, overlapping to make a firm surface which would resist blows, sword thrusts and the piercing of arrows.

The drawbacks of mail as a protective covering ulti-mately started to become more evident, especially when knights had to contend with the effects of the longbow (see

Armed soldiers carrying out the Massacre of the Innocents, *c.* 1250. Add. MS 17687 B.

Et pscebat figuram dm nrm ihm xpm
qppm e rex q̃ oia regna tralit
Sic em ⁊ sardos q̃ pma missa relebuit
Melchisedech rex ⁊ sardos pane ⁊ vinu obtulit
Sub speie panis ⁊ vini ho primern instituit
Cua pro sardos Et oinez melchisedech uocabat
Cuia primcen por oblacoe melchech psigabat
Melchisedech erat sardos ⁊ Epuceps regni
Ino pulche insignabat dignitas pdotat
Sardotes ber pua diri principes inpiales
Excellat E impates padauchos ⁊ pucipes
Et cera qamo ipans unlect anglicas
Sardotes em parimta oficiut q̃ angli fac nequiut
Ut maranche ñt ihsz ola pato portne
Emana E pncxpalig dei pat ola tranaba
... cuia famlitudine tussima

page 59). Even when doubled for extra strength, mail broke easily and was liable to be pierced by arrows travelling at speed, not to mention being prone to rust and difficult to clean. Initially protection was improved by adding pieces of metal plate or hardened leather to shield vulnerable parts of the body (see page 43), at first just the knees and elbows, but subsequently the legs as well. By the early fourteenth century, elbow-guards, greaves – the gutter-shaped plates defending the shins – and knee cops were all to be found in common use. Solid plate offered far better protection than mail because it was virtually impenetrable by arrows or sword points and could also spread the force of a heavy blow. At first solid breastplates began to appear under or over the hauberk, initially made of hardened leather, but later of iron. Sometimes the mail hauberk was supplemented by a form of body armour known as a pair of plates, consisting of a fabric or leather garment lined with overlapping pieces of metal, rather like a scale hauberk turned inside out. Where the breast section was a single plate, the skirt either retained the pair of plates construction or was made of narrow horizontal hoops allowing the wearer flexibility to bend. By this time reinforcing plates on the limbs had spread to include the upper arms, forearms, shoulders and thighs, whilst a series of small overlapping plates protected the front of the foot, and scale reinforcements were added to the mail gauntlets which superseded the earlier mittens (see opposite). The appearance of the knight was completed by a short, sleeveless surcoat, more practical for combat than the long flowing garment previously worn, and suitable for displaying the wearer's heraldic arms.

A knight in full armour kneels before a king, 1436–38. Egerton MS 878, f. 37.

De Polibetes ne conuoites
Les armes tlz soient malortes
Car au despouller densuiuta

By the early fifteenth century plate defences were completed by the introduction of a backplate to match the breastplate, causing the surcoat to go out of fashion. Gauntlets were strengthened by the addition of metal strips to protect cuffs and fingers, while elegant pointed steel shoes had a single plate enclosing the heel at the back and a series of overlapping narrow metal bands for flexibility at the front. Defensive body armour had now reached a point at which the wearer could rely almost totally on an outfit made of hinged and riveted plates for protection, although a miniature in an early fifteenth century manuscript of a knight being armed for war suggests that mail may still have had its uses, not least as lightweight protection for his horse (see page 48). Further developments became mere modifications to maximise efficiency. Plates were made larger so that fewer were necessary and, thanks to the constantly improving skills of the armourers, better shaping and closer fitting offered maximum resistance to missiles and blows. By the end of the century the defensive quality of body armour had reached the point at which no further improvement was possible without making armour so heavy that mobility would be seriously impeded.

The helmet, standard equipment for a mounted warrior, was worn either as a reinforcement for the mail coif or on its own. Early helmets were conical, sometimes with a bar riveted onto the rim as a nose-guard, a feature still in evidence in the thirteenth century. The knight portrayed on pages 56–57 wears a simple round-topped helmet of a type appearing towards the end of the twelfth century at the same time as a new flat-topped style that was to develop into

A heraldic knight, *c.* 1410–14. Harley MS 4431, f. 137.

aymon ton loyal coufin   tevta xxvbi

the characteristic all-enclosing helm of the thirteenth century (see pages 50, 51). Deep and more or less completely cylindrical in form, it often curved in towards the throat at the front. Reinforced 'sights' or slits were provided for the eyes, and small holes at the lower part of the front allowed the wearer to breathe. Although of formidable appearance, its flat top was a natural target for heavy blows which could stun the wearer, and by the end of the century the shape had again become conical to create a glancing surface that would deflect heavy blows rather than absorbing them.

Even with eye-slits an all-enclosing helm would have had considerably impaired vision, so from the fourteenth century the section covering the face was given pivots to allow it to be raised, either for a better view in action or when combat was not expected. This movable face protector, or visor, was also fitted to a new lightweight helmet known as a bascinet, developed from the simple rounded steel skull cap worn by many knights throughout the thirteenth century in preference to the cylindrical helm. At first the visored bascinet retained a rounded shape, but soon the top was modified to become conical. The visor had a sharp, pointed swelling over the nose, giving the knight a particularly distinctive appearance. At first bascinets were worn over the built-in coif, but later the throat and neck were protected by a tippet or aventail, a miniature mail cape attached to the bascinet and sometimes buckled or tied to the body armour to stop sword or lance thrusts from passing underneath it. From an early stage the tippet might also be covered by a plate collar, but with the more widespread use of solid metal protection it was common for two or

Arming a knight, *c.* 1410–14. Harley MS 4431, f. 112.

**Mail-clad knights with
flat-topped helms,**
13th century.
Royal MS 12 F XIII, f. 11v.

Two knights in combat in an
amusing bestiary illustration
to the entry for 'horse',
13th century.
Royal MS 12 F XIII, f. 42v.

Ca est la vengeance du gnic Roi alixandre

more gorget plates to be worn over the tippet, fixed in such a way that the lower edge of the visor fell inside their upper edge. Pointed visors could still be found, but a version with a blunt swelling over the nose and mouth became more usual, and helmets were shaped to fit the contours of the head, giving them a more rounded appearance.

Frequently manuscript miniatures depict warriors in helmets with a rounded top and narrow brim, strangely reminiscent of modern military wear. Known as 'kettle helmets' on account of their resemblance to an upturned cauldron or medieval 'kettle', they first appeared in the twelfth century and remained popular throughout the Middle Ages. Even when worn over a coif they offered inferior protection in combat by comparison with their enclosed counterparts, but they must have been far more comfortable to wear. Such helmets were also extremely valuable for certain types of siege work such as mining, since vision remained unimpaired and the brim could deflect descending missiles.

The knight's other distinctive feature was his shield. The large round shield which protected the body in earlier times was impractical for mounted combat. A knight on horseback could use his sword to defend his right-hand side, but he could very easily be trapped with the entire length of his left-hand side exposed. This led to the introduction of a long kite-shaped curved shield with a rounded top, which screened the body and most of the left leg. Such shields, made of leather-covered wood and bound with steel bands, had a strap or 'guige' which went over the neck and round the right shoulder to support the shield fully when not in

A king and his knights wielding swords in battle, *c.* 1340. Royal MS 19 D I, f. 47.

use and reduce weight on the left arm when needed in action. Later the shield's rounded top became straight, presumably for better vision, and in about 1250 a smaller 'heater-shaped' shield, formed like a downward pointing triangle with curved sides, was introduced. Rapidly increasing in popularity, it remained in use until body armour had been strengthened to the point where a shield became an unnecessary encumbrance.

Medieval knights gain some of their colourful reputation from the heraldic devices that they display (see page 46), heraldry partly owing its origins to the introduction of the face-concealing helm which made it impossible to distinguish friend from foe in battle. By the mid-twelfth century some knights carried shields painted with distinctive devices which were later to reappear on the shields of their sons. From these early stages an elaborate system of identification developed in which small variations were devised to distinguish younger sons and branches of families. The devices used were generally animals, birds or simple geometric shapes, bold enough to be recognised at a distance. The shield was the most prominent place for heraldic identification, but an armed and mounted knight had other opportunities to display his device. It could be painted on the surcoat worn over the hauberk – hence the term 'coat of arms' – and on the saddle cloth or horse trapper. Armorial devices were also displayed on flags. The ordinary knight's flag was a pennon, pointed or swallow-tailed in shape, and carried at the top of his lance. Higher-ranking knights or commanders bore their arms on banners, at first rectangular and attached lengthways along the lance, but later almost square.

The knight's most important piece of fighting equipment was his sword, supplemented by a dagger or other weapons which might contribute towards success in military encounters. He also carried a lance, to be tucked under his arm and used in the charge. Highly prized as a possession that passed from father to son in Saxon times, the sword commanded a veneration that developed a symbolic role in the Middle Ages as a token of knighthood. The early sword had a long, straight, two-edged blade with a deep groove down the centre to reduce the weight without weakening the cutting edges. The handle or hilt was separated from the blade by a short protective crossbar, while the grip terminated in a heavy knob or pommel which helped to counteract the weight of the blade. Although modifications were made to deal with improvements in the protective quality of body armour, the basic design of the straight two-edged sword remained unchanged throughout the Middle Ages. At first intended merely for slashing, the blade began to be made longer, slimmer and with a better point so that it could also be used for thrusting. The introduction of solid body armour prompted the appearance of special swords with blades forming a diamond shape in section and tapering to a sharp point, particularly effective both for thrusting between the joints of plate armour and for piercing mail. Many knights carried such a sword in addition to a dual-purpose sword for cutting and thrusting. Solid body armour may also account for the introduction of a longer and heavier sword with a deep hilt, which could be wielded with both hands to give greater striking power. Manuscript miniatures from the thirteenth century onwards portray warriors using a falchion, a sword with a broad, cleaver-shaped blade curved at the cutting edge (see below). Generally wider at the end nearest the point, the distribution of weight along the blade gave it exceptional shearing force. Less common than the straight-edged sword, it still enjoyed a certain amount of popularity.

A giant armed with a falchion is defeated by a knight, end of the 13th century/beginning of 14th. Royal MS 10 E IV, f. 304v.

4
ARMIES AND BATTLE

With no concept of a regular army in the Middle Ages, almost any man could find himself involved in military action. Knights, wealthy enough to equip themselves with armour, weapons and a horse, rendered military service in return for the possession of land, whilst foot-soldiers came from the poorer classes. The only body armour they could afford was usually homemade – a quilted tunic or gambeson – sometimes with a helmet or other piece of armour that they had been lucky enough to find on the battlefield. Frequently they fought with axes, clubs or whatever they could lay hands on to serve as weapons, but their ranks also included the archers, an extremely significant force in military engagements, particularly in the later part of the medieval period.

The longbow, used by foot-soldiers, was a fast-shooting long-range weapon of great impact and importance. Although capable of accuracy if carefully aimed, its chief strength in battle lay in its suitability for massed attack. A

An encounter between archers on the battlefield, *c.*1420–30. Arundel MS 67, f. 144.

le bucuw a　　　　montaufnes et se muc

volley of arrows fired by a comparatively small body of archers might easily destroy a charge by a much larger group of mounted knights. The longbow, which first appeared in the English army after Edward I had seen it in action in Wales in the late thirteenth century, rapidly proved its worth and became a decisive factor in many of the battles of the Hundred Years' War. The crossbow existed earlier, rising to prominence in the twelfth century. It consisted of a short, heavy bow, powerfully sprung and attached at right angles to a stock which performed the same function as the arm of the longbow archer. Mechanical devices were used to span the bow, which was too stiff and powerful to be spanned by hand (see opposite). It was long-range, hard-hitting, efficient and deadly accurate, but slow and cumbersome to use. For a long time regarded as the ideal infantry weapon, it finally lost its superiority when the longbow appeared, chiefly because it just could not compete with its rival's rapid rate of fire.

A miniature showing a fifteenth-century army on the march in winter (see page 62) demonstrates how progress might be hampered by adverse conditions – here a heavy snowfall. Moving an army from one place to another was a challenging manoeuvre at any time of year, as the country was rough, the roads were poor, and accurate maps just did not exist. Wagons were the only means of transporting all the paraphernalia of a fighting force in transit but they frequently caused a hindrance to an army's progress by breaking down on the uneven terrain. Although food could normally be secured en route by means of scavenging, looting or pillage, there was at the time no viable alternative to moving the principal part of the force's equipment in this way.

Spanning a crossbow during a fierce battle, 1473–80. Royal MS 18 E V, f. 54v.

lui deffendurent et lui dirent
quil laissast ceste chose ester et
que ce nestoit pas sens de fo
lie encommencer ne de mettre
soy en aduenture si grande si
le bouterent les sacres et puis
sans hommes de la ville hors
dicelle pour euiter a lincon
uenient qui de tele entreprise
pouoit aduenir

lux ducs
desperez q̄
z estoient
auoient il
de comme
noble cite
u auoit
ent pour
tout leur
z et tollu
fuuent ete.
ouuut tost
france et
r les chips
e preudho
chartres.
au soleil
ont en au
ne quilz
et plus
mez eto.

A large army comprised three main divisions or 'battles', each consisting of cavalry supported by a body of infantry. When marching they adopted the order of van guard, main guard and rear guard, but on the battlefield the divisions were deployed in a number of formations according to the situation in hand. An encounter with the enemy might start with preliminary skirmishes of outriders and perhaps some crossbow fire as the armies manoeuvred into position, each hoping to tempt the other into making an impetuous assault with a disastrous outcome for the aggressor. When an attack finally began it took the form of a succession of charges section by section, thus ensuring the continuous application of pressure even if one group failed and needed to retreat to reorganise. Charges were made by separate units, each containing thirty to forty knights grouped round a leader's flag and using a common battle-cry for mutual encouragement in the assault. Although medieval battles now conjure up images of colourful banners, spirited charges and deeds of bravery, the lack of discipline in most medieval armies undoubtedly led to a great deal of brutality and bloodshed (see pages 12–13, 73).

Battles would have been extremely noisy with the thudding of horses' hooves, the clash of weapons and armour, the whirring of arrows and the shouts of the participants. A battle-cry was probably distinguishable amidst the general uproar where reliable comprehension of a leader's verbal commands would have been impossible. The need for an alternative means of transmitting orders led to the development of military music, nowadays an activity in itself, but formerly a vital element of battlefield action. Various

An army on the march in winter, 1479.
Royal MS 17 F II, f. 116v.

Troops in battle formation,
c. 1470–80.
Royal MS 16 G IX, f. 76v.

**Two armies come face
to face,** before 1483.
Royal MS 18 E I, f. 269.

A military encounter on foot.
c. 1420–30.
Arundel MS 67, f. 341v.

(above)
**Confrontation of two armies in
battle,** 1332–50.
Royal MS 16 G VI, f. 219.

(opposite)
A victorious army, *c.* 1485–90.
Yates Thompson MS 32, f. 5v.

(overleaf)
A hostile encounter on a bridge,
after 1380.
Royal MS 20 C VII, f. 137v

Et la medi enfuiuant. xiiij. iour
du dit mois de nullet le dit regët

fut lost moult estonne car les autres esto
ent venuz acourant et soudainement. S
valerent pluis les vns qui et les autres

(above)
**A group of foot soldiers defeat
an unarmed enemy,** after 1380.
Royal MS 20 C VII, f. 133.

(opposite)
Fatalities in battle,
c. 1479–80.
Royal 15 E I, f. 273v

(opposite)
**Using the terrain to
best advantage,**
c. 1468–75.
Burney MS 169, f. 111.

(above)
In the thick of battle, *c.* 1415.
Cotton Nero E ii, part 2, f. 152v.

instruments – horns, pipes, drums and particularly trumpets – were employed to produce melodic calls to indicate commands or identify centres of resistance, as well as generally intimidating the enemy with their noise. Some military musicians wore armour, but many miniatures depict them as unarmed, even when performing at the heart of the action.

Purpose-built fighting ships were unknown in the Middle Ages. In times of war fishing craft and merchant vessels were organised into fleets, and every sailor was forced to become a soldier when the need arose. Although not designed for fighting, a medieval ship might be converted into a 'man-of-war' by erecting wooden towers at each end and fastening a fighting top, a structure sometimes resembling a large barrel, at the highest point of the mast to serve as an observation post or provide height for the archers. A miniature of around 1480 (see pages 80–81) shows a fleet of converted vessels attacking a seaport, whilst another illustration depicts two ships engaging in a military encounter on the open sea (see page 82). In a naval battle two ships came as close together as possible, allowing the occupants to fire arrows at their opponents and attempt to board the enemy vessel, a grappling hook being carried specifically for this purpose. Once aboard they engaged in hand-to-hand combat (an undertaking fraught with danger in itself because of the confined space) until one side had overpowered the other. The outcome decided, the victors usually threw their opponents overboard unless they were important enough to command a ransom.

A fleet of ships carrying soldiers sets sail,
1470–72.
Harley 4379, f. 60v.

nble et retournerent tout ainsi
antihoie les trois chevalliers
ssus nommes se tindrent sur
r place les trente tours tout
mplie et oultre prise sen retour
rent tout par loisir chascun en
lieu. Quant ilz furent venu

le duc de thourime et les seig
a xxxe qui leur furent bonne ch
re ce fut bien raison car mout
vuillamment sestoient porte
grandement avoient garde lh
neur du royaume de france co
bien y paru au iousts. IIII

emprinse z du boyage des ch
liers francois et des chevaliers
flois et du duc de bourbon qui
fut chief de larmee a la reqste
tennenoir pour aller en bar
pour assegier la forte ville

saincte et noble emprinse qui se
en celle saison de chevalliers de f
ce et dangleterre et dautres pay
oultre mer ou royaume de barbe
Et ne la vueil ie pas oublier n
aucunement laisser darriere n

(left)
Warships on the move,
before 1483.
Royal MS 18 E I, f. 103v.

(overleaf)
Attacking a fortified town by sea,
c. 1480.
Harley MS 326, f. 29v.

dunkerque Nous les eschaperons
bien. Les aucuns se confortoient
sur les parolles du chld et les
autres non. Touteffoiz se misrét
ulz en ozdonnance de deffence Si
sappareillerent Arballestriers po̅
traire et canons pour gecter.

(opposite and above)
Hazards of warfare at sea,
late 15th century.
Royal MS 14 E IV, f. 276 &
Royal MS 16 G VIII, f. 317

(opposite)
An army on the move,
c. 1480.
Harley MS 326, f. 90.

(above)
Taking a hostage, 1380–92.
Yates Thompson MS 35, f. 246.

Comment la ville de Ribodane fut prinse de force par les Anglois. Le chapitre.

Nuiron quatre Jours aprez ce que messire Jehan de hollande / et messe Thomas de persi furent venus en lost du mareschal / Et quilz eurent Cheualiers et escuiere auec toutes manieres de gene ordonnez a vn appareil dassault Aprez plusieurs euures faictes

la ou on vouloit / et dedens cellui pouoient bien aisement / Cent archiers et autant de gens darcs qui eust voulu / mais pour cest assault archiere y entrerent / Et auoit on remempli le fosse alendroit ou lengien deuoit estre menez — Lors commença lassault et lengien a aprochier la ville legl aloit a force de boutemens sur

5
CASTLES AND SIEGES

Sieges were preferable to pitched battles and skirmishes in the open field since the latter were far more likely to be costly in terms of loss of men and equipment. In addition, armies were expensive to maintain and there were difficulties involved in moving a body of soldiers from one place to another. A far less risky campaign could be conducted by undertaking a succession of sieges to capture enemy strongholds that controlled the countryside around them, which meant that a knowledge of siegecraft was an essential requirement for every military commander.

Development in styles of military architecture in the Middle Ages owed much to progress in the field of ballistics and other forms of attack - the more efficient the weapons and methods used in sieges, the more modifications to strongholds were necessary to resist them. Assaults might involve towns and cities, generally fortified with walls and other defensive features such as a moat, but siege warfare was particularly associated with the castle, an important

Siege techniques and equipment,
c. 1470–80.
Royal MS 14 E IV, f. 281v.

An army marches on a defended city, *c.* 1405.
Burney MS 257, f. 166v.

feature of the feudal system in Europe which reached England with William the Conqueror. Although designed as a fortress, the castle was also the residence of its lord and symbolised his wealth and power.

Early timber castles were built on a flat-topped mound of earth (the motte), connected to an enclosure (the bailey), the whole site being protected by a system of deep ditches and earthen ramparts surmounted by wooden palisades. This general plan remained, but fire-resistant stone soon replaced the timber structures. The rectangular stone keep, a distinctive feature of eleventh- and twelfth-century castles, was certainly more resistant to attack, but sheer strength was not enough. Despite its formidable appearance there was a weakness – it had sharp corners, easy to undermine – which prompted the appearance of round tower keeps in the early thirteenth century. By this time a stone curtain wall was also being constructed round the site, not only as extra protection for the keep but also to offer defenders a wider field of fire. Soon defence shifted from the keep and curtain walls were modified accordingly. Built higher to discourage scaling by ladder, they were given towers curved to the field to maximise coverage of the ground beneath. The weakest point of this arrangement, the entrance, was protected by a strong gate-house flanked by high towers and often equipped with a drawbridge and portcullis (see page 92). Further elaboration produced concentric castles, the culmination of medieval design, where the provision of second, lower curtain walls created a double line of defence and counter-attack, offering a model

**Using a siege tower for
observation**, 1332–50.
Royal MS 16 G VI, f. 280v.

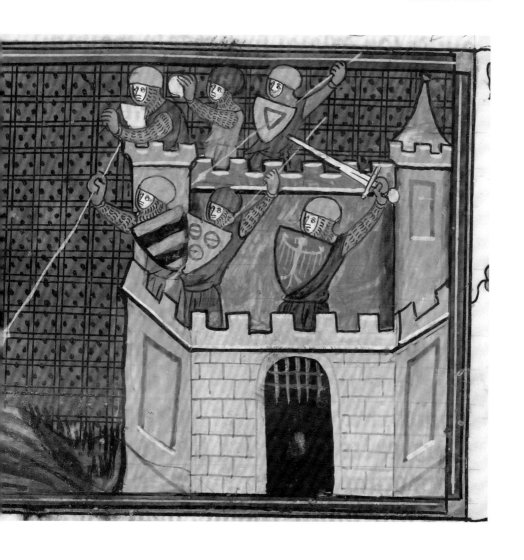

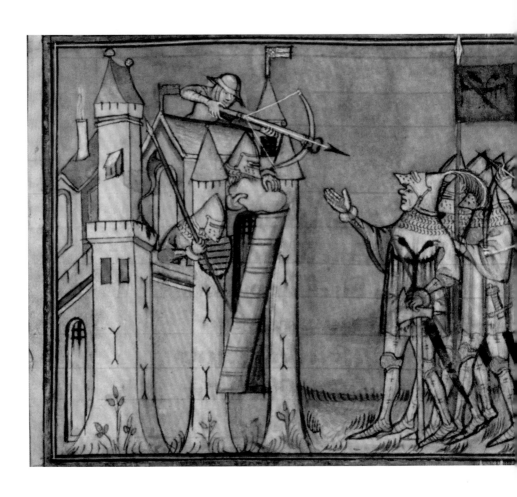

The leader of the besieging army attempts to parley with the opposition, *c.* 1380–92.
Yates Thompson MS 35, f. 51.

for the updating of many existing structures through the addition of an outer wall.

Siege warfare utilised a wide variety of skills and weapons. If initial diplomacy failed, an attempt would be made to enter the stronghold and gain control by means of hand-to-hand encounters. The image on page 96 shows one method of achieving this, an assault by a scaling party using tall ladders (also see page 116). Highly effective if well supported by covering fire, escalade was also an extremely dangerous activity as defenders could dislodge the ladders or hurl down stones or other heavy missiles. An account of the life of Bertrand Duguesclin, a fourteenth-century French knight whose courageous deeds earned him legendary fame, recounts that at one siege he fell some considerable distance into the moat when knocked from his ladder by a descending stone. Although lucky enough to survive on this occasion, his image was almost certainly ruined when he had to be dragged out unceremoniously by his heels.

The diversion created by the escalade can provide cover for a sapper, otherwise unprotected as he attempts to breach the base of the castle wall, but better protection is provided if sappers can carry out their work under cover of a movable shelter (see page 98). An initial breach either preceded further destruction with a ram or was the first stage in undermining the foundations of the castle, an operation greatly feared by defenders because it was virtually impossible to counter. At a point where the structure was most vulnerable a cavity was hollowed out in the base of the wall, underpinned with wooden stays to avoid premature collapse and packed with combustible material. When this was

(opposite)
Crossbow in use at a siege,
late 14th century.
Royal MS 20 C VII, f. 24v.

(above)
Crossbows to the fore,
1232–61.
Yates Thompson MS 12, f. 204.

Ous auez bien
cy dessus ouy
recorder coment
ladmiral de fra
ce atout trant routte de
gens darmes arriua ou la
ure de handebourt en escoc
de Et comment ses gens
trouuerent autre pays et
autres gens guilz ne cudoi
ent. les barons descoche et
le conseil du roy lannee

lautres de bonnes gens dar
mes et v. arbalestriers et
euffent auecq culx leur ha
nois darmes pour culx bien
armer auecq celle ayde et
le demourant descocde ilz c
batterient bien les anglois
et ferwient vne si grant
tion en angleterre q iama
ne ferwit recouure. Sur
cest estat auoient ladmiral
de france et les francois pro

ignited the stays caught fire and collapsed, bringing down the wall above. Such mining activity was sometimes concealed by starting operations under cover at a distance from the wall and tunnelling under the foundations. Defenders were totally helpless against such an attack, unless they could manage to dig a countermine and gain access to the besiegers' tunnel for a hand-to-hand engagement.

(opposite)
Entering a captured castle,
before 1483.
Royal MS 18 E I, f. 345.

(above)
Scaling and mining in a siege,
1332–50.
Royal MS 16 G VI, f. 118v.

Scaling, mining and other attempts to gain entry might be successful in their own right, but a castle could also be surrounded and attacked by means of bombardment. Arrows were ineffective against stone masonry so huge engines, derived from those of classical antiquity, attacked the stonework and intimidated defenders by hurling dangerous or unpleasant missiles into the besieged area. Earlier machines, very rarely illustrated in manuscripts, were either

**Mining under cover of a movable
shelter,** 1325–50.
Royal MS 16 G VI, f. 74.

a kind of giant crossbow relying on the principle of tension for propelling its missile, or a sort of catapult, sometimes identified as a mangonel. This was a wooden frame with a twisted skein of springy material stretched between its sides, through which was inserted a revolving arm with a hollow at one end for the projectile (see page 104). The missile-carrying end of the beam was winched down and released, the twisting action of the skein bringing about the firing of the missile.

The third type of machine, a medieval invention simpler than its earlier counterparts and more powerful, worked on the pivot principle. The trebuchet, portrayed in a detailed and convincing way in an illustration to a manuscript of an Arthurian romance made in the early fourteenth century (see page 106) had a sling at the longer end of the arm, while a box containing a heavy weight was attached at the other end. Thanks to the force of gravity the counterweight dropped when released, causing the arm to revolve and the sling to be tossed outwards and upwards to discharge its projectile. The trebuchets employed in sieges appear to have been of massive size, generally much larger than earlier stone-throwing machines, and with a longer range.

(overleaf)
**Cannon and crossbows
in use at a siege,** 1470–72.
Harley 4379, f. 83v.

Cannon and ammunition ready for use, *c.* 1470–80. Royal MS 14 E IV, f. 28v.

Q̃nt les barruns ceo ourent del Toiu̅ s̃c Auale
S̃ eignurs d̃it Rollant p̃ dieu de couleste
A eu̅s̃ uulis qe mū cor̃ps̃ suit er̃.xxx. lues po
B̃ en̄ en c̃est̃e Toui̅ estre lapide

pres le mois oyuer qnt li soues

(opposite)
Preparing to operate a trebuchet,
early 14th century.
Egerton MS 3028, f. 106.

(above)
**'Mangonels' in use
at a siege,** c. 1300.
Bibliothèque Nationale.
MS Fr. 2824, f. 94v.

(above)
Firing a trebuchet in the siege of a castle, *c.* 1316.
Add MS 10294, f. 81v.

(opposite)
Trebuchet attended by four soldiers, 1326–27.
Add MS 47680, f. 43v.

nantibus. Et ergo spes eorum: spes est fidu
cia uictorie et quolibet utriusque: quorum cor
pus est coniunctio utriusque partis. Quando
ergo non inacuit spes uictorie. De se ipsis mon
unt uir et cessant prelia. Et perdurat prelium:
quam diu durat perseuerancia in spe superandi.
partem qualibet utriusque. Sit ergo conatus
tuus et intentio tua: in durabilitate et perseue
rantia tui. Et in stabilitate et sustentatione
illorum qui sunt tui generis. Et non uilipendere
personas illorum quasi contemptor. Set col
lige uerba eorum. Promitte eis donaria et ho
nores: et solue promissa. Scias itaque quod
non oportet te intendere in exercitu: nisi toga
tum uel togatum. Sit ne subito inueniaris
ab inimico: te querente. Sit magna solici
tudo tua et prouidentia tua in premunitione
tui ipsius. Scilicet. Custodibus. Et explo
ratoribus. Et necessaria est uigilantia in
quolibet tempore noctis et diei. Et noli me
tiri castra nisi in loco iuxta montem uel conueni
to est. Uel iuxta aquas. Et confer uictualia
a multa gentili: quamuis non indigeas to
ta die. Et multiplica machinas diffidenti

moꝛe ⁊ maioꝛe ad acquiretis laudem
⁊ honoꝛem · Ẽdte nobiliſſime do
mine · ſi p̄ miſſa · de gueris ⁊ cõflictibꝫ
obſeruetis cõmiſſa · Et aua deb̃
lis ⁊ imonibꝫ igitis · nobili regi ale
ãdꝛo de macedonea tiarũ ꝛ̃iſtoꝛii · pꝛ
philoſophũ ariſtotilem · philoſo
ploꝛũ pꝛincipẽ quõdã ɛdita · ſi in libꝛo
de ſecꝛetis ſecꝛetoꝛũ ⁊ pꝛudencia ꝛegũ ple
nius fuit ɛtẽta ⁊ p̄ me uob̃ miſſa ꝛr̃
mia gero fiduciam · q̃ t aduitus in terre
equeſtuut honoꝛẽ ⁊ gr̃am · Et in cel
ꝛegnando cum deo ⁊ tota celeſti mili
cia · gloꝛiam ſempiternam · Qued
reus concedit qui ſine fine uiuit
⁊ ꝛegnat · Amen.

6

GUNPOWDER AND THE DECLINE OF MEDIEVAL WARFARE

The innovation responsible for challenging and finally transforming medieval warfare practices was gunpowder, which opened up the way for new, more powerful types of weapon, capable of achieving a far more devastating impact than that of their traditional counterparts. Thought to exist in the thirteenth century, there is no evidence of the exploitation of gunpowder for warfare purposes until about the mid-1320s. A reference to a cannon appears in the ordinances for the city of Florence of 1326, and the first known pictorial representations occur at about the same time. An illustration in a manuscript in the library of Christ Church, Oxford, has achieved international fame as the earliest surviving picture of a cannon (see opposite). It shows a primitive vase-shaped gun, loaded with a bolt and lying without restraint on a trestle table, with one figure in attendance, igniting it at the top. The volume, a treatise on the duties and obligations of a king by Walter of Milemete, King's Clerk and later Fellow of King's Hall, Cambridge, is

A gunner ignites a vase-shaped cannon, 1326–27. Christ Church Oxford, Western Manuscripts, MS 92, f. 70v.

one of a pair of manuscripts executed in 1326–27 and intended for presentation to Edward III. Its companion, a treatise on the education and duties of princes attributed to Aristotle, is preserved in the British Library and likewise contains a representation of a cannon, also showing a primitive, vase-shaped gun, lying on a massive frame and loaded with a long-headed dart. In this case four figures are in attendance, one of whom ignites the weapon through a touch hole at the rear or breech end, level with the mouth. In both cases the artist must have been unaware of the cords needed to lash the gun to the frame – the force of the explosion would almost certainly have caused a free-standing gun to recoil, killing both gunner and bystanders.

The unusual 'bottle' shape of this cannon probably ensured that the section where the gunpowder actually exploded was the strongest part of the weapon. A very early vase-shaped gun found in Sweden indicates that the barrel inside was cylindrical as in a modern gun. The earliest cannon, cast in brass or copper, fired feathered darts or quarrels, but rapid improvements in size and shape soon led to the use of heavier and more damaging projectiles made of lead and stone. Towards the end of the fourteenth century, when the 'bottle' shape had been replaced by a cylindrical form with one end closed by an iron chamber for the powder, cannon started to be constructed from longitudinal strips of iron welded together, with iron hoops driven over them from end to end. Many early cannon were comparatively small, such as the early fifteenth-century piece depicted opposite, which has a complex shape consisting of a short thick barrel and a rather longer and narrower

A cannon and crossbows at a siege, *c.* 1415.
Cotton MS Nero E ii, part ii, f. 1.

chamber with a broader rim at the rear end. Again the artist does not seem to have understood the technical workings of a cannon – it is apparently firing a stone missile without the aid of an attendant gunner and without emitting any smoke – but the portrayal of the weapon itself may well be based on accurate details, as two similar guns of Italian origin have survived.

Although often fired directly from ground level, supported by timber framing at the sides with a wooden support let into the ground at the breech end to prevent recoil (see pages 100–101), early cannon could also be positioned on wooden stands to which they were secured by means of leather thongs, ropes, strong wire or iron bands. The same small piece described above is mounted in this way. It lies in a shaped bed on a stout horizontal wooden beam mounted on vertical and diagonal supports, to which it is fastened with a metal strap passing over the chamber towards the rear end, presumably nailed down to keep it secure. At the rear the narrower part of the beam passes between two parallel wooden bars tilting backwards, possibly acting as some kind of primitive elevating device. In an illustration of a castle being closely attacked on all sides (see opposite) the two cannon in the foreground also sit on shaped and sloping wooden beams, mounted on strong wooden stands, but without any sign of straps or fastenings. The cannon to the left is apparently equipped with some kind of elevating device at the rear to enable the beam to pivot on its frame and improve the range. Elevating quadrants used with free-standing wooden supports normally took the form of a curved wooden or iron upright with a number of holes to take a

Extensive use of cannon for assault on a castle, *c.* 1490-1500. Harley MS 4425, f. 139.

fixing pin so that the end of the beam supporting the gun could be secured at the desired angle. Attacking at close quarters, the gunners in the foreground shield themselves from attack by means of sturdy curved shields, whilst the gunners attacking from the rear are protected by wooden mantlets or shelters, custom-built with an opening to take the barrel of the firearm. Cannon used on fixed stationary supports like those illustrated must have been awkward to transport or construct *in situ*, so it is hardly surprising that wheeled gun carriages soon made an appearance and rapidly became very widely used (see opposite).

Alongside the cannon shown in the illustrations we sometimes see armed figures equipped with handguns, another development arising from the use of gunpowder (see page 116). First appearing in the later part of the fourteenth century, these guns were conceived as a kind of miniature cannon with a long wooden handle attached to a short brass barrel. The defending gunners in the illustration are firing with the weapons resting on their shoulders for taking aim, but handguns might also be operated by holding under the arm. Firing was achieved through a touch hole at the top of the barrel, either by using a piece of burning slow-match held in the gunner's hand or with a piece of wire, red-hot at one end.

As a propelling agent gunpowder was far superior to the forces of tension, twisting and gravity on which the firing of traditional weapons had relied, but neither cannon nor handgun achieved the instant success that might have been expected and they took quite some time to become established as serious rivals to the weapons that they finally

Two small wheeled cannon on the battlefield, *c.* 1479–80. Royal MS 15 E I, f. 47.

displaced. In hindsight this is hardly surprising as the handling of gunpowder must have been extremely dangerous in the early days. Primitive cannon were not only inaccurate to fire and cumbersome to move and manoeuvre, but also highly unsafe in themselves because they were apt to fracture and burst unexpectedly. James II of Scotland met his death during the successful siege of Roxburgh in 1460, not as a consequence of enemy action but as the result of an exploding siege cannon. Contemporary accounts vary in their descriptions of the exact circumstances, but one reports that at the time the cannon was merely being prepared to fire a welcoming salute to James's queen, Mary of Guelders, who was about to arrive during a break in the proceedings.

Despite its early problems the introduction of gunpowder was to signal the beginning of the end for traditional medieval warfare. Although typical medieval weapons continued for quite some time in parallel with their gunpowder-fired counterparts the advantages of exploiting the superior power of gunpowder soon became apparent. As a result the necessary technology was gradually developed to construct cannon and handguns that were both safer to operate and more powerful in their effect. The gradual spread of these new weapons of combat not only gave a fresh dimension to traditional military encounters, but also introduced a mechanical and impersonal element to combat that was ultimately to bring about a complete change to the face of warfare as it had been experienced in the Middle Ages.

(opposite)
Escalade and firepower used for an assault on a castle,
1487.
Royal MS E VI, f. 22.

(overleaf)
Attacking a city,
c. 1400.
Stowe MS 54, ff. 82v–83.

nauer qui sauuase ne seorvt
troie de plus pres Adont se
uindrent les autres uesses
lessees et abessees et coui
urent au port toille des leuees
la ot grant noise et ny ot
sigaudy qui neust paoms
et quant ils orent abaisse
leurs soilles et leurs ness
furent encores les troies
les assaillirent qui leur
y ssue deffendirent Deulx
des ness surent en traume

saus cdaube lessees et traui
stespessent que monte
otrstuent des troiens si
plue de mil en thauenu
mors e pasmes sur le sa
blon et par force les sta
tecoiles auec grant multi
tude de troiens y suront
qui leur suront y suront
villenue si se cosondren
ensumble ayoult le sit
bien prothesclans et si
gtucreusement se comur

**Weapons old and new
are used side by side,**
late 15th century.
Royal MS 14 E IV, f. 59v.

FURTHER READING

The text of this book has been compiled to provide context to the illustrations. Numerous detailed books on the subject of medieval warfare are available of which the following may be of interest.

Matthew Bennett,
The Medieval World at War,
Thames & Hudson, 2009

R. Barber
The Knight and Chivalry,
Boydell Press, 2000

C. Gravett,
Knight: Noble Warrior of England,
1200–1600,
Osprey, 2010

J. Bradbury,
The Medieval Archer,
Boydell Press, 2014

J. Bradbury,
The Medieval Siege,
Boydell Press, 2008

K. S Nossov
Ancient and Medieval Siege Weapons,
Lyons Press, 2012

Sean McLachlan,
Medieval Handgonnes,
Osprey, 2010

Terence Wise
Medieval Heraldry,
Osprey, 1980

The Osprey series of books on warfare. (Many individual items relating to war in the Middle Ages)

(opposite)
A victorious army returns home,
before 1483.
Royal MS 18 E I, f. 12.

(overleaf)
Confrontation of the English and French armies,
c. 1415.
Cotton MS Nero Eii (part 2), f. 40v.

INDEX

Numbers in italics refer to illustrations

A

accolade 29
aketon 42
archers 59, 61, 76; *4–5, 59*
architecture, military 87–93
armour 9, 25, 27, 32, 39–57, 59, 76; *44*;
    see also under individual items
army 18, 28, 59–85, 88, 92; *18, 63, 68,*
    85, 88, 92
Arthurian 99
aventail 49
axes 59

B

backplates 47
bailey (castle) 89
banners 55, 63
bascinets 49
battle-cry 63
battles (army divisions) 63
Bellifortis 21, 23; *21, 23*
body armour 39–47, 49, 54, 59
breastplates 45, 47

C

cannons 109–14, 117; *99, 103, 109, 110, 114*
castles 87–97, 106, 113, 117; *97, 106, 117*

chivalry 25–26
clubs 59
coifs 42, 47, 49, 53
collars, plate 53
crossbows 61, 63, 99; *61, 95, 99, 110*
crusades 21
curtain walls 89

D

daggers 55
De re militari 17–18
diplomacy 93
Duguesclin, Bertrand 93

E

Edward I 61
Edward III 110
elevating devices (for cannon) 113–14
escalade 93–97; *117*

F

falchion 56, *57*
flags 54–55, 63
foot-soldiers 9, 42, 59, 67, 72
Frontinus, Sextus Julius 18

G

gambeson 42, 59
gate-house (castle) 89
gauntlets 45–47

gorget 53
greaves 45
Guelders, Mary of 117
guige 54
gun carriages, wheeled 114; *114*
gunpowder 109–10, 114, 117

H

handguns 114, 117
Hastings, Battle of 11; *11*
hauberks 40–41, 45, 54
helmets 39, 40, 47–53, 59
heraldry 47, 54; *25, 47*
horse armour 47
horsemanship 27
horse trappers/saddle cloths 54

J

James II of Scotland 117
jousts 31–32, 36; *32, 36*

K

keep (castle) 89
kettle helmets 53
knee cops 45
knights 9, 18, 25–32, 36, 39, 42, 45, 47, 49,
    50, 51, 53, 57, 59; *6, 9, 25, 26, 31,*
    36, 38, 45, 51, 53, 57; arming of *49*;
    heraldic *47*; mail-clad *40, 50*;
    mounted 25, 27, 40, 54–55, 61; *27*
knighting ceremony 28

L

lances 25, 49, 54–55
longbows 45, 59, 61

M

mail (armour) 40–45, 47, 49, 50, 55; *40, 50*
main guard (army division) 63
mangonels 99; *105*
manuscript miniatures 10–11, 18, 27, 39,
    47, 53, 56, 61, 76
mêlée 31
Meun, Jean de 17
Milemete, Walter of 109
military manuals 15–23
military music and musicians 63, 76
military training 15, 27–28, 31
mining (of castle walls) 53, 89, 93, 97; *97, 98*
mittens, mail 42, 45
motte (castle) 89
musical instruments (drums, horns,
    pipes, trumpets) 76

N

naval warfare 16, 76–83

P

pennons 25, 54
plate armour 42, 45, 47, 53, 55
plates, pair of 45

R

rams (siege engines) 16, 93
rear guard (army division) 63
Roxburgh, siege of 117

S

sappers 93
scale armour 42, 45
shields 25, 27, 39, 40, 53–54, 114
ships 76, 79; *76, 79*; *see also* naval warfare
siege machines 87, 97–99; *see also* mangonels,
siege towers, trebuchets
siege towers 15; *90*
siegecraft 15–16, 17, 87
sieges and siege warfare 18, 53, 87–93, 95,
    97–99, 117; *87, 95, 97, 99, 105, 106, 110*
slow-matches 114
squires 27–28; *27*
Strategemata 18
surcoats 45–47, 54
swords 25, 27, 29, 31, 53, 55–56, *53*; cutting
    and thrusting 42, 49, 55; effectiveness of
    armour against 45, 55

T

'technical' illustrations 15–17, 18, 21
tippets 49, 53
tournaments 9, 31–32; *32, 36*
trebuchets 99; *21, 23, 105, 106*
trumpets *see* musical instruments

V

van guard (army division) 63
Vegetius (Flavius Vegetius Renatus) 17–18, 27
visors 24–25, 26

W

wagons (for army equipment) 61